Edoardo Erba was born in Pavia near Milan in 1954. He studied at the University of Pavia and at the Piccolo Theatre in Milan. His plays include *Radical Obstruction*, *The Night of Picasso*, *Wild Boar*, *Human Tissue*, *Blind Corner*, *Marathon*, *Gronchi Rosa*, *The Family Vice*, *Third Millennium*, *The New Year's Eve of the Millennium*, *The Man of My Life* and *Salesmen*. His work has been performed at the Teatro Erba, Turin, as well as at some of Italy's top festivals: the Venice Biennale, the Taormina Festival, the Montepulciano Festival and the Tuscolane Festival. *Marathon – Maratona di New York –* was first produced in Parma in 1993, having won the *Premio Candoni* the previous year, and has been produced in Barcelona and Buenos Aires, while *The Night of Picasso* and *Wild Boar* have been produced in Los Angeles at the Stages Trilingual Theatre. Erba has also written for cinema and most notably television for which he has written dramas, sketches and sit-coms. He lives in Rome.

Edoardo Erba

MARATHON

English version by
Colin Teevan

OBERON BOOKS
LONDON

WWW.OBERONBOOKS.COM

First published in 1999 by Oberon Books Ltd
521 Caledonian Road, London N7 9RH
Tel: +44 (0) 20 7607 3637 / Fax: +44 (0) 20 7607 3629
e-mail: info@oberonbooks.com
www.oberonbooks.com

A catalogue record for this book is available from the British
Library.

PB ISBN: 9781840021394

Visit www.oberonbooks.com to read more about all our books and to buy them.
You will also find features, author interviews and news of any author events, and
you can sign up for e-newsletters so that you're always first to hear about our
new releases.

Contents

Introduction

(This dialogue took place via email during 1999, between Belfast and Rome.)

Teevan: Edoardo, the Anglophone world only gets occasional glimpses of Italian theatre. The three playwrights whose work has been widely translated and produced in our theatres this century are Luigi Pirandello, Eduardo de Filippo and Dario Fo. Do you believe there have been any major developments or trends in Italian playwrighting in the generation that has followed Dario Fo?

Erba: De Filippo and Fo seem to us to be too 'regional', above all because of the language they use. Pirandello isn't so loved by the new generation. His themes aren't so obvious or relevant, and he is considered a 'boring classic' of our century. In my opinion Ancient Greek theatre, Shakespeare, Goldoni, Beckett and the American movies of the sixties and seventies have had much more influence on myself and my contemporaries.

Teevan: How and where would you place yourself in contemporary Italian theatre?

Erba: I believe that I am largely an anomaly. Although I have read widely in Italian literature, it has not been a great influence. In fact, only Fo has made a lasting impression on me and that largely due to his ability to communicate the comic spirit of his theatre. Kafka, Pinter, Ionesco, Jung, Borges and Dino Buzzati – a wonderful Italian writer little known abroad – these are my masters.

Teevan: While there are, for want of a better word, 'realist' elements in the various writers you mention, none of them would be seen as 'realist' writers per se. Do you consciously avoid an exact mimetic realism?

Erba: I have never succeeded in writing pure realism, because when I imagine a story it spontaneously seems to locate itself upon that jagged line which separates reality, dream and vision. Some people have said to me: why not write a realist story? Quite frankly, because it seems to me that our 'real' lives are lived on this very line.

Teevan: Do you find yourself drawn to particular themes and styles of theatre?

Erba: I am interested in themes of death, God, love, family and social justice. I love sport and science also as sources of inspiration; above all, physics and biology. Although I no longer have faith, I remain 'religious', though I'm not sure God would agree with such a paradox. I have a spontaneous sense of the comic both in the theatre and in life. I laugh a lot. I would like to cry more sometimes, but I can't. Above all I produce plays to entertain the public. I would like to reflect the changes current in Italy.

Teevan: Do you feel Italy is changing?

Erba: From abroad Italy appears a country with a precise identity. I think it was true for my grandfather's generation. Nowadays my country has lost part of its identity, inevitably a result of the power of the new global culture. You can feel this process in two ways: negatively, because it destroys the preceding forms; positively, because it forms a new taste – for example, it gives an Italian the possibility to appreciate Blues or Soul, or a Londoner the chance to see plays by someone like me!

Teevan: Or, indeed, us a chance to have this electronic dialogue. You have written a dozen or more plays, what would you say characterises your writing?

Erba: It reflects my character. I cannot stand being bored, so I try not to encourage it in my audience. I believe that writers have a capacity to bore, but not the right. Sure, some of the greats earned the right to bore –Tarkovsky, for example, is extremely boring but with him the pain of boredom is worth it. This is my primary rule of writing. I also re-read a thousand times. I suffer from depression so I cannot stand stagnant situations. The only way out of these situations is through originality and, if an idea does not surprise me with its originality, then I reject it.

Teevan: Do you approach the writing of all your plays in the same manner?

Erba: As with all writers some of my plays are written in very short spaces of time, others take me perhaps a year to finish and, at that, only after ten drafts. Plays are like children. They are all different. One causes you no end of difficulties and problems, another is no bother whatsoever, but at the end of the day you cannot say which one gives you the most satisfaction. I look to write in a simple, clear way. This is not the way I speak. I speak very poorly, I hesitate, go off on tangents, I can't remember words and I 'eh' a lot. I try to avoid this in my writing.

Teevan: You have written over a dozen plays in addition to your writing for other media. Do you consider yourself to be a prolific writer?

Erba: As you say I have written a dozen plays but this is over a period of ten years. I don't know whether to say I have written too many or too few. Sometimes I feel that I am lazy. Other times, by contrast, I feel that I should go out and live a bit more. I love all my plays and when I re-read them I find them beautiful. Except one. *The New Year's Eve of the Millennium* for which I won a prestigious award but which I frankly find a bit shoddy.

Teevan: When I first read *Marathon* I felt it was such a perfect play; a strong, apparently simple piece of dramatic action, the central metaphor of which resonates on so many levels. Our casting director on this first production has described it as 'a little tangerine of a piece' (in case you get the wrong idea I believe she means that she feels it is a peach of a play only smaller and more vivid, or perhaps it is a miniature version of Hawking's – or was it Einstein's – description of the shape of the universe as an orange that is turned inside out again and again in ever increasing proportions.) Anyway, what I was wondering was whether you are aware of all the levels of a piece as you are writing it?

Erba: My original idea for *Marathon* was to have two actors running on the stage. I discovered myself that jogging with a friend you chat a lot, and the subject of the conversation is often determined by your physical situation at the moment. But this was just an idea. Yes, the characters are running and speaking, but what can happen in the play? I was thinking about that, when I happened to hear a secretary in a theatre telling the story of a young actor who fell into a coma after an accident. He was not a friend of hers, but they found only the telephone number of the theatre in his pocket and called her. So the girl spent the night near him, speaking and speaking. I wondered how her voice could be received by the boy in the coma? *Marathon* was born.

Teevan: Do you analyse your work after it has been written or, moreover, produced? Do you reflect upon its importance and how you achieved certain effects?

Erba: When I'd finished *Marathon*, everybody told me: it's a great play. But it is good for a writer not to know whether he has written an important work, or whether he has yet to get there. It is also better not to analyse your work because then there will be the tendency to imitate yourself. I find that I follow an internal thread and it turns into a play only if the idea corresponds with the emotion that I am living at the moment. For these reasons some ideas remain there for years. I notice that recently I have been drawn towards older characters in my plays. This must mean that I am getting older.

Teevan: As I said earlier, you have written a lot for television. Would theatre be your first love – as a medium? And do you find that different media enable you to explore different subjects?

Erba: Theatre continues to be my first love. But I think it is a good experience for a playwright to write for television, because you can understand better the nature of contemporary mass-communications. A human being who goes to the theatre is an active subject, a real live individual who will switch off if you aren't able to interest them. Working for TV you begin to think that there aren't 'people', but 'categories of people'.

Teevan: What category of person is your theatre aimed at?

Erba: Good question.

Teevan: I notice that you yourself translate work from English to Italian. Most recently Patrick Meyer's *K2*. Do you think a play can ever be translated?

Erba: I don't know. You must try and try again and judge the result of your efforts.

Teevan: The more plays I have translated, the more I have come to the conclusion that there are as many translations of a single piece as there are translators. I firmly believe that there is no such thing as an exact translation because to translate exactly, or literally, kills the spirit of the piece. I feel it is the job of the translator to create a corresponding world in the receiving language in which the spirit and impact of the original can be recreated. Do you have any theories on the process of translation?

Erba: Yes. Fortune. You have to be lucky and find the right key to enter a text. And the author has to be lucky with their translator!

Teevan: Well... (*Pause.*) Finally, Edoardo, have you ever run a marathon?

Erba: No. Just a half-marathon (21km) four years ago.

Teevan: And did you feel like half an Athenian?

Erba: No, but I had just had the flu!

Acknowledgements

I would like to thank not only Edoardo Erba for both his original text and his continuing interest in the process of rendering it into English, but also Mick Gordon for instigating that process and his reflection and constructive criticism throughout, Dr Paula Magill for her comments on my initial Italian translation, the actors Stewart Graham and Richard Dormer whose generosity with their time, performances and comments were much appreciated, and finally, Gillian Hanna.

Characters

MARK
early twenties

STEVE
early twenties

This English version of *Marathon* was first performed at the Gate Theatre, London, on 18 November 1999, with the following cast:

MARK, Ciaran McMenamin

STEVE, Benjamin Waters

Director, Mick Gordon

Designer, Dick Bird

Lighting design, Neil Austin

Sound design, Paul Arditti

Music, Gary Yershon

Note: This playscript went to press before opening night and therefore may differ slightly from the text as performed.

Night-time. A country lane, near a town or city.

MARK, lit by the light of the moon, is stretched on the ground, barefoot. He wears a tracksuit top and a pair of old football shorts. He appears to be sleeping.

STEVE enters. He is dressed in running gear: jogging shoes, cycling shorts and singlet. He wears a stopwatch. He carries a pair of old tennis shoes in his hand which he throws down near to MARK.

MARK rouses himself and slips the shoes on.

MARK: I'm fucked.

STEVE: Hot tonight.

MARK: I'm sweating like a cunt.

STEVE: Like I said.

MARK: How long's it been? Two weeks?

STEVE: Eight days.

MARK: I'm full of shit.

STEVE: Yup.

MARK: My body is full of shit. Only finished the antibiotics yesterday. Took so much cough medicine my blood's practically treacle. (*Coughing.*) Much good it did me –

STEVE: We going to do it or aren't we?

MARK: We're going to do it. It was me who insisted we do it. I've got to run this shit out of my system.

STEVE: I could have been watching the telly.

MARK: There's never anything on telly.

STEVE: The match.

MARK: Oh yeah, the match. Fuck. But why watch the match when you could be out here beholding the glory of nature?

STEVE: It's night. You can't behold a thing.

MARK: The smells. Behold the smells of the natural world –

STEVE: Behold my arse.

MARK: No thanks.

MARK and STEVE do exercises to stretch their muscles.

STEVE: You ready?

MARK: Listen, let's take it easy. We know we can do the level crossing in twenty-six, so what does it matter if it takes us forty tonight. Eh? We could even walk for a bit to begin with –

STEVE: Why don't we look for mushrooms while we're at it?

MARK: There's an idea –

STEVE: We either do it well or don't do it at all.

MARK says nothing.

Last chance to chicken out –

MARK: The chicken never crossed my mind.

STEVE: Once we start, there's no turning back –

MARK: Until the level crossing that is –

STEVE: Until the level crossing –

MARK: So, what are you waiting for?

STEVE: Fuck off. (*Adjusting his shorts.*) I'll set the pace. Let's try and break thirty tonight.

STEVE starts his stopwatch and starts running.

Come on!

MARK: (*Stopping him.*) Hang on.

STEVE: What now?

MARK: The Volvo. Did I lock the Volvo?

STEVE: (*Stopping his stopwatch, annoyed.*) Yes, you locked the Volvo.

MARK: (*Confused.*) Yeah. Yeah, course I locked it –

STEVE: (*Starting his stopwatch again.*) Now come on!

They both start running. Long silence.

MARK: How long?

STEVE: Fifty-seven seconds.

MARK: We set off a bit fast.

STEVE does not react.

First minute's the cunt. The shock to the system. The desire to stop's at its strongest.

STEVE: Well talk, then. Talking helps.

MARK: I can barely breathe. Fuck. I just had the fucking flu, remember.

STEVE: Do you think the guy in Ancient Greece who ran from Marathon to Athens worried about the flu? Not likely. Not with the Persians advancing – a sea of the bastards – flooding the plain of Marathon and just him and eight thousand nine hundred and ninety-nine Greek mates standing between them and Athens itself.

MARK: I expect that held his attention.

STEVE: Well, they won all the same. Nine thousand against a million, or thereabouts – thanks to their superior tactics. But then, after the battle, which had been raging all day, the general says to this guy: take a message to Athens, tell them we've won, tell them they're saved. Twenty-six miles, three hundred and eighty-five yards! Does it bother him? Does he stop to worry about suitable convalescing period from any recent minor ailments? He does not. Off he goes, runs the whole thing, non-stop; straight to the marketplace where he shouts, 'We won,' and then drops dead. That guy's my hero. What was his name?

MARK: Your story, not mine.

STEVE: We should study the Olympics at school instead of Pythagoras and Euclid and their triangles and theorems. There's more in the Olympics than in all of maths and philosophy. I mean, look at us, doing something that has no sense, knowing it has no sense, but doing it to the bitter end all the same. It's just like life, when you think about it. They understood these things, the Athenians.

MARK: Glad someone did.

STEVE: A different race altogether!

MARK: Wish they'd invented a different race altogether. Fuck.

STEVE: Do you have to curse so much?

MARK: Yes, I fucking do. It's a mental expectorant. Clears my mind.

STEVE: You find it cathartic?

MARK: I find it supercocksuckingly cathartic.

STEVE: You're feeling a bit better?

MARK: I'm feeling a bit weirder –

STEVE: Breathing or legs?

MARK: Both. My lungs feel like a flushing toilet. My legs feel like – like shite.

STEVE: It's all the medicine you take.

MARK: Fucking antibiotics.

STEVE: You take too much medicine.

MARK: I only took what I was meant to take. Fucking doctors.

STEVE: You've always taken too much medicine –

MARK: What do you know about always? We only see each other to go running, spare me the lecture.

STEVE: You're always on something; cough medicine, codeine, this, that, the other – you're a fucking mess.

STEVE pulls away effortlessly. MARK struggles to stay behind him.

MARK: You know, I must have seen the back of your neck a thousand times. It's the part of you I know the best. It's how I'll always remember you. It's the window to your soul. Your fucking neck.

STEVE: Overtake me then.

MARK: Why should I, when I can gaze upon your soul back here. It's not a pretty neck, you know. In fact, it's quite a dull neck, entirely lacking areas of special interest or scenic beauty. It's the neck of a robot.

STEVE: I love you too.

MARK: I hate necks. It started with Piacentini's neck. He was this kid I knew. Spots, overweight, midget. You'd have liked him, the little bumfucker. When I was a kid my mother'd never let me out on my bike. I was desperate to go out but she always said no. She was afraid of the traffic, she said. Took a whole month just to get permission to go to the end of the street. For my birthday the following spring she let me out for two hours as a special treat. Do you know what those two hours meant to me? A race with Piacentini. A race to the death. I telephoned him, we were to meet at the roundabout. The time comes, and he's there waiting, but I'm so excited I go too fast and can't stop in time and my pedal hits his wheel – ting – I snap one of his spokes. I'm sorry Piacentini, I say. I'm going home, he says. But I said I'm sorry, I say. And you've loads of spokes, I say, your bike still works, you can still race. But no, he says, the wheel's slightly warped. But the race, Piacentini – but he's already turned his bike and started for home. Leaving me there, on my own, staring at his pustule-pocked neck. I hated that neck.

STEVE does not react.

I should have smashed his head in. Why didn't I smash his head in? Fucking idiot. I should have gone after him on the bike and given him one in the face.

STEVE: He must have been bigger than you.

MARK: No – I've never really reacted. I boil with rage inside, but then – nothing. When I was kid I was an altar boy. One time, in the sacristy, after a mass, with this other kid, Mascherpa, and we were arguing – can't remember what about – but we were nose to nose and saying 'Yeah!' 'Yeah?' 'Yeah you prick!' 'Prick? Me a prick?' 'Yeah, prick!' 'You calling me a prick, you prick?' 'Yeah. Yeah, I am, prick.' The way you do. All the others

make a circle round us. And it's like I
see the whole thing in slow-motion. And
I say to myself: right, now, give him one
in the face. But while I'm thinking this,
he gives me one in the face. And I begin
to shake. Rage, fear – I don't know. But
I'm shaking. And Mascherpa sees I'm
shaking and he starts to imitate me. And
the others start to laugh. And I feel a
bit dazed, and I should do something.
I should at least walk away. But I can't.
Because while I'm thinking I should walk
away, Mascherpa walks away. And all the
others. Leaving me there, on my own,
again.

STEVE shakes his head.

I'd like to run back in time and smash in
all those heads I should have smashed in
before. How long?

STEVE: Eight minutes, fifteen.

MARK: You hurting?

STEVE: Yup.

MARK: Should have said so earlier. It helps
me to know you're hurting.

They go on running in silence. MARK shivers.

Humid tonight.

STEVE: Heard the forecast? Widespread frost!

MARK: Frost my bollocks! We're both sweating like a pair of cunts!

STEVE: Speak for yourself.

MARK: Well, I'm sweating like a pair of cunts.

MARK shivers.

Though now you mention it, I am beginning to feel a bit colder.

STEVE: You're pathetic, you know that?

MARK: No, really, I feel cold and sweaty all of a sudden.

STEVE: That's normal.

MARK: Normal my arse! I don't want to have a relapse.

STEVE goes on undaunted.

How long is it now?

STEVE: Ten minutes.

MARK looks around.

MARK: But where are the safety bollards? We usually pass the safety bollards after ten minutes.

STEVE: We're slower tonight. Got to speed up if you want to see the sights.

STEVE speeds up. MARK tries to stay in behind him, but STEVE is flying.

MARK: (*Out of breath.*) I can't, I'm not firing on all cylinders. You go on, I'm turning back.

MARK turns and runs in the opposite direction.

STEVE: What the hell are you doing?

STEVE, in his turn, turns, follows him and catches him up.

You can't give up. You're talking too much, that's all. Okay, we'll do it your way, go at your speed. We can take it down a gear. If it takes more than thirty to the level crossing, fine, we can make it up on the way back. Come on.

They both turn and start running again in the original direction.

MARK: If I catch pneumonia, it's your fault.

STEVE: You'll definitely catch it if you stop.

Pause.

As long as you're moving you're fine. But as soon as you stop you've got to cover yourself. If you stand around half-naked in the cold air –

MARK: Someone could fuck you up the arse.

STEVE: I was at The Skorpio – in the sauna –

MARK: Oh yeah?

STEVE: Fuck off. A friend of yours, a girl, wanted a word. I was in great shape. I thought I was some kind of Greek god or something. Indestructible. So I come out of the sauna and look at myself in the mirror and I'm sweating –

MARK: Like a –

STEVE: I'm sweating like someone who's been in a sauna. And as I look at myself I think: I'm indestructible. And I say: to hell with it. I leave and go straight to the gym's café and have drink with her, your friend. What an idiot. I go home and then it hits me, the fever. I call the doctor: straight to hospital; x-rays; the works. He says it's bronchial pneumonia. Four weeks in bed, laid up. And I never even got to, you know –

MARK: Fuck her up the arse?

MARK giggles. Stops.

Which 'girl-friend' was it, anyway?

STEVE: Probably for the better. The vagina's a notorious source of infection.

MARK: Mental infection. Women – you leave yourself exposed to them and they infect your mind –

STEVE: Like a virus that destroys the logical processes.

MARK: Their victims turn into gibbering, insane shadows of their former selves –

STEVE: And die.

They run for a bit in silence.

How you doing?

MARK: Bit better.

STEVE: You're like a diesel engine, the more you warm up, the better you run.

MARK: I'd run even better after a little break.

STEVE: You know we've never tried going for two hours.

MARK: Two hours?! Did you hear what I just said?

STEVE: We don't know if we can do it.

MARK: I don't want to know if we can do it.

STEVE: We don't even know what's beyond the level crossing.

MARK: I don't give a fuck what's beyond the level crossing.

STEVE: Well, why not find out what's beyond it?

MARK: We already agreed; the level crossing and back.

STEVE: But tonight I feel we really could do something.

MARK: Yeah, some serious damage to ourselves.

STEVE: After an hour you don't feel it so much. You enter a whole different dimension.

MARK: You enter it if you want. I'm happy where I am.

STEVE: When we get nearer the crossing we'll see how we feel.

MARK: What about the safety bollards?

STEVE: What about them?

MARK: We haven't passed them yet.

STEVE: We must have passed them.

MARK: I didn't see them.

STEVE: It's dark.

MARK: I have never not seen the bollards. Never.

STEVE: Calm down and keep your pace steady. And lift your head up. If anyone could see us they'd think we're two sorry bastards.

MARK: No shit!

MARK rummages in all of his pockets.

The keys?

STEVE: What about the keys?

MARK: I don't have them. If I locked the car, I must have the keys. Did you take them?

STEVE: Nope. You must have left them inside.

MARK: But if you're sure that I locked it –

STEVE: Doesn't matter. Keep your concentration.

MARK: Well, how will we get back inside if it is locked?

STEVE: Stop worrying and keep going. We can always break a window. Hot-wire it –

MARK: Hot-wire your bollocks! That's my old man's car. Do you know how much a Volvo costs? He doesn't even know I took it.

STEVE: One thing at a time. Okay? Now's the time for running. You need your energy for running. So forget about the keys and run.

MARK: Let's turn back, Steve.

STEVE: (*Changing tack.*) Everytime it's the same. Looking for excuses to turn back – your antibiotics, the bollards, the bloody keys – for once and for all you are not turning back, right?

They run for a bit in silence.

MARK: The more I think about it, the more I think this running thing is just a little bit in danger of becoming one big pain in the arse. What are we trying to prove? Women don't seem to find it necessary to prove themselves. Sure, there are women who run –

STEVE: Lesbians.

MARK: That's what I like about you, you're so broadminded. What I mean is that women –

STEVE: (*Interrupting him.*) I'll tell you about women. It's not that they can't run, or that they can't handle the exhaustion, it's that they can't see the point of it all. They say: what's the point in running today? And when you say: because yesterday I did it in thirty, today I want to do it in twenty-nine, they say that that's no reason to do it. Have you ever watched a fight on the telly with a woman? Why are they hitting each other? she says. Why does this one hit that one, she says. Because if this one hits that one, then that one's just going to hit this one back. That's what she says because that's the way a woman's mind works. They just don't get the point of it all, they just don't get it, why we do the things we do, the way we do. And you say, just look at it, for Christ's sake, just look at the fight.

MARK: Yeah, just look at the fight, you stupid cunt.

STEVE: Yeah!

MARK: Yeah!

They laugh.

So, why are we running?

STEVE: New York. The marathon. November coming. Remember?

MARK: Oh yeah.

STEVE: The tickets are booked. No turning back.

MARK: We'll need five hours running in our legs.

STEVE: Five or six.

MARK: How long have we been going?

STEVE: Twenty-two minutes.

Silence.

MARK: Do you know, sometimes I think
women have a point

STEVE: Why did the Greek guy decide to
run twenty-six miles, three hundred and
eighty-five yards? He said: I have to run
it, so I'll run it. Of course, I could take
a rest, he said to himself, no-one will see
me take a rest, but even though I could
take a rest, I'm not going to take a rest.
I'm going to run, he said to himself. You
know, when I see a guy out there who's
not prepared to suffer, I say to myself this
guy's a – a wuss.

MARK: Easy, you might hurt his feelings.

STEVE: A wimp.

MARK: Oh, please stop, I can't take any more!

STEVE: A wanker, a tosser, a complete
spineless morally feeble fucking coward!

MARK: That's better.

STEVE: It's not a question of physique
– I'm not talking about that – it's that

you won't get anywhere if you're not prepared to suffer. It's something women don't understand. There's a logic which eludes them.

MARK: Maybe they're not the only ones.

STEVE: If there's a fight, what do you do? Run away?

MARK: Like fuck!

STEVE: Well, it would cross your mind. And if it did, and if you ran away, how would you feel?

MARK: *If* I did, I'd feel like a coward, I suppose.

STEVE: Exactly like a coward. It's the same as football. When the opposition are all over you, you've got to have nerves of steel. You've got to mark up, stick tight, close down the gaps. You've got to dig deep, soak up the pressure and take it like a man and then, maybe, nick a goal on the counter. That's what my old man says about football, because there's nowhere to hide on a football field. Football will always find you out, he says. You can't wing it, you just can't fake it.

MARK: Women can fake it.

STEVE: Women don't play football.

MARK: Yes they do.

STEVE: Lesbians –

MARK: Of course. And of course lesbians don't have to fake it because they don't have to bother worrying about the brittle male ego. Not that the brittle male ego really cares whether the woman comes or not, he's just hoping that if she came then she mightn't have noticed that he wasn't really caring whether she came or not or, indeed, paying any attention to her at all the entire time and that a belated show of interest combined with her coming might give the impression that he cares that she came. So what team does your old man support, then?

STEVE: Inter.

MARK: Talk about lesbians!

STEVE: They were the kings of Europe.

MARK: The carpet-munching kings.

STEVE: That's my dad's football team you're talking about.

MARK: Well, I shit on your dad's football team.

STEVE: Well, I shit on your dad's football team. What is your dad's team?

MARK: Inter. Don't worry, everyone shits on Inter. AC've been at it for twenty years.

STEVE: Inter were unbeatable in the sixties.

MARK: Unbeatable! A bunch of Scottish part-timers beat them in the '68 European Cup Final.

STEVE: Glasgow Celtic are not part-timers.

MARK: They are a bunch of bald, beer-bellied, inbred, sheep-shagging, Sunday footballers. I've seen films about the Scottish.

STEVE: Glasgow Celtic are a good team. Were a good team. Besides, that final was a fluke, a one-off – my old man says. You could tell from the start of the match, he says. When they were lining up and the camera panned across their faces, he says he knew they'd lost. They were too wound up to get into it. You can always see from the start who's going to win, my old man says. It's written in their eyes. If you're calm, if you're sure of yourself, your opponent doesn't interest you. You rely on yourself. You know you can do it.

MARK: I'm not so sure I can do it. Tonight.

STEVE: Too late. Now we're up and running, the crowd are cheering, we can't disappoint them.

MARK: Nobody'll know us in New York –

STEVE: The Italian-Americans, they'll know us, they'll recognise us. They'll be waving to us and shouting, 'Go, go, go.' Don't you hear them?

MARK: Steve, we're not in New York –

STEVE: It's all the same. Christ! Don't you understand? Every time you run you need to have the same attitude, the same determination, the same perseverance. Because that day will be just like this. You'll want to give up, like you want to give up now. And if you give up now, you'll give up in New York.

They run for a bit in silence.

MARK: Steve?

STEVE: What?

MARK: Do you think God exists?

STEVE: Sometimes you get on my tits, you know that?

MARK: Sometimes I have my doubts.

STEVE: Well, don't doubt it, because you really do get on my tits.

MARK: By our age we should have decided if He exists. Or at least if He exists for us. But we always put off deciding definitively whether or not He exists?

STEVE: Have you decided anything definitively about women? About work? About having kids? You've decided nothing definitively. So, why decide definitively about God? And why tonight?

MARK: When I was little I believed in Him.

STEVE: Because He brought you presents at Christmas.

MARK: No, I really believed in the one true holy Roman and apostolic God. At night, before going asleep, under my covers, I'd pray to Him. I was sure He heard me. I'd ask Him things, like not to let me get another two for conduct on my report card –

STEVE: Your family's a bunch of religious maniacs.

MARK: What do you know about my family? You've never even met my family. Apart from my sister –

STEVE: She's cute, your sister.

MARK: Shut up about my sister. What do you know about my sister? I bet you can't even remember her name –

STEVE: Paula –

MARK: How come you remember her name?

STEVE: Because she's cute.

MARK: Shut up about her. She's not cute.
She's one big pain in the arse. And she's
far too good for the likes of you.

STEVE: Nice breasts. Round, firm, juicy.
Like nectarines –

MARK: You disgust me, you know that, you
have a filthy fucking mind and absolutely
no sensitivity. A brother does not want
to listen to shit like this about his sister, a
brother does not want to think about his
sister's breasts, a brother does not want to
think of his sister as anything other than
a pain in the arse whom he must protect
from his badass friends whose minds he
knows to be shit-filled sewers of filthy
imaginings. So shut the fuck up about
my fucking sister. We were talking about
my family of which she is an atypical
member, my family whom you have not
met, my family about whom you know
absolutely nothing –

STEVE: I bet your mother's cute too.

MARK: You know, I'll kill you, I swear I'll
fucking kill you –

STEVE: I know everything about your family. Every time you open your mouth, you talk about your family, or when you were little. Of the things you did, the things you said when you were little. And I'll tell you this for nothing, no-one gives a damn about when you were little. You were just one more little bastard like the rest of us little bastards.

MARK: How the fuck did we ever become friends?

STEVE tries to speed up to get away from MARK, but, unexpectedly, he has difficulties.

What is it?

STEVE: My spleen.

MARK: Is it a sharp pain?

STEVE: What other kind of pain is there?

MARK: I don't know – dull, throbbing, unbearable, excruciating –

STEVE: It's sharp.

MARK: Like a stitch. It'll soon go, you'll see. Used to happen me, when I was little, when I'd run. I was always running. My mother would say, slow down, Mark, you're always running, you'll hurt yourself –

STEVE: It's unbearable –

MARK: Sorry, was I talking about when I was little again?

STEVE: The pain is unbearable.

MARK: Take a deep breath. Then breath out. All the air. The secret's to get all the air out –

STEVE: I do not have a problem with my breathing. My spleen hurts. It's fit to burst. I can feel it against my intestine –

MARK: Well then we should stop. If only for a minute.

STEVE: Like fuck we're stopping, I'd rather it burst.

MARK guffaws with laughter.

I don't see what's so funny.

MARK: 'Marathon man in burst spleen bloodbath.'

STEVE: So? It would be just like the story. People would remember me like they remember the Greek guy.

MARK: Whatever his name was. Marilyn: suicide. Presley: drugs. Bogart: cancer. Steve: spleen.

MARK laughs.

STEVE: John Lennon: shot dead. JFK: shot dead. And you, you bastard, if you don't shut it.

MARK: Being murdered's not the most mythic way to go. For me, it's the car crash. Life in the fast lane. James Dean in his Porsche. Wham bam –

STEVE: Princess Diana –

MARK: Here, why didn't Superman rescue Princess Diana – ?

STEVE: I don't know.

MARK: Because he's in a wheelchair!

STEVE: You're sick, you know that?

MARK: You're not much better yourself. (*Pause. He laughs.*) James Spleen!

MARK laughs. STEVE joins in reluctantly. They are soon laughing so much that they have trouble continuing.

For God's sake let's stop!

STEVE: We are not stopping. (*Contorted, shouting more at himself than MARK.*) Run, for Christ's sake, run! The worse you feel, the more you must run, run away the pain, run away the tears. Go on, move your legs, you bastard, move your arms, get into the myth.

MARK: Whatever.

STEVE: Well then, go, go, go... ahh (*Presses his spleen.*)

MARK: What is it?

STEVE: It's like a knife in my side.

MARK: Let's stop. It's only meant to be a bit of fun –

STEVE: Fun! Fuck! It's going to hurt and hurt and then hurt some more. But even if it hurts, you keep going. I'm not going to New York for a stroll.

MARK: It's months away.

STEVE: We must train like it's tomorrow.

MARK: Steve, if this is getting like a job, forget it –

STEVE: It's much more than a job.

MARK: That's not how it was at the start.

STEVE: It's never like that at the start. It might even have seemed like a bit of fun at the start. But you don't achieve anything if you're not prepared to sweat blood for it.

MARK: But why? Like when your mother says finish your dinner and you say you're not hungry and she says you've got to finish it anyway and think of all the starving children. So you stuff yourself sick in the name of starving children everywhere. What kind of logic's that? Why put yourself through something you're not up to? You don't want to do. It's not natural. It's not being true to yourself.

STEVE runs on, through his pain.

How you doing?

STEVE does not respond. They run. MARK appears to hit an obstacle and falls. The other is forced to stop but continues running on the spot.

STEVE: What the hell you doing, you idiot?

MARK: There was a stone, or something, and I fell –

STEVE: (*Checking his stopwatch.*) Okay, but now, back on your feet, we're losing precious seconds.

MARK: I can't.

STEVE runs on the spot for a few moments then relents.

STEVE: Christ! (*Stopping his stopwatch. Stops jogging on the spot.*) Right. Where does it hurt?

MARK points to his ankle.

Just a sprain. Let me see.

STEVE kneels, he takes MARK's leg and, like an accomplished physio, gives it a quick jerk.

You didn't shout.

MARK: Should I have?

STEVE: (*Grabbing him by the T-shirt.*)
You've done nothing, you stupid bastard.
~~You only want to take a rest.~~

MARK: I only want to make you take a rest.
I want you to make it home with your
spleen intact.

STEVE: You worry about your spleen, right?
I'll worry about mine. Now, come on.

MARK: This is no good. I want to feel free.
We can run till we drop dead, fine, but we
should also have the choice to stop. If we
want to. That way we can still do it. Still
get there in the end and yet we are, by
the same token, free –

STEVE: Don't try and Zen your way out
of this. You know damn well that if you
choose to stop for a minute, you'll never
get there. At the end of the day, running's
a question of overcoming your fear –

MARK: Why is it always a question of something else? Why can't it just be a question of running?

STEVE: That's your problem, you question too much. You shouldn't question. You should just run. I'm going to run.

STEVE restarts his stopwatch and starts running. MARK follows him.

MARK: You're such a cunt to me sometimes, you know that!

STEVE: No-one's forcing you.

MARK: It's always the survival of the fittest with you. There's no philosophy, no beauty –

STEVE: That's what it's about, life: survival. And only the fittest survive.

MARK: But we have brains, intelligence. We can sometimes choose to serve something other than narrow self-interest. Otherwise we'd be like animals –

STEVE: We are like animals. We are animals. And weak animals die, fit ones survive.

MARK: But with our intelligence we can affect the laws of natural selection. With intelligence we've developed things like medicines. With medicines it's not only the fit who survive –

STEVE: Sure, the old, the sick and the handicapped survive too and that leads to overpopulation, and too few people paying taxes supporting too many people who are dependent on the state which in turn leads to poverty. Look at the streets. Look at all the homeless –

MARK: Yeah! Shoot the bastards!

STEVE: At least I'm more honest than hypocrites like you, who give them a thousand lire at traffic lights to bugger off. How's that going to help 'affect' things?

MARK: What do you know about what I do at traffic lights?

STEVE: I can just imagine you. You stop at the lights in daddy's Volvo, you roll down your window, you might even give them a smile –

MARK: Not always. Sometimes I'm also capable of your *Mein Kampf* reasoning. Like I say to them: what do you want? I've already given one thousand lire to your colleague. Colleague! What a cunt am I! The other day this one kept insisting: cup of tea mister, spare some change for a cup of tea mister. I took out my wallet, and he kept it up; cup of tea mister, spare some change. I said to him, you shut the fuck up with your fucking cup of tea or I'll give you sweet fuck all, that's what I'll give you. But it was the tone of voice I said it in –

STEVE: If he was getting on your tits –

MARK: I was ashamed. I once thought there was a natural justice. I don't know anymore.

STEVE: Life's just naturally a vale of shit and man but a prisoner therein.

MARK: Through the valley of shit He leadeth me, no evil shall I fear... so why make it even shittier for ourselves? Why bust our guts – ?

STEVE: To give it one up the arse. That's why I'm doing it. To fuck life up the arse. Fuck it. Fuck life. It fucking stinks from start to fucking finish. That's what you've got to remember, that's what you've got to keep fixed in the forefront of your mind, or you'll never get through it. Life's a fucking nightmare. And you are fucking in it. And you must fuck it up the arse, before it fucks you – which it's fucking going to do, mark my words. So before that day you must make it pay, pay for being a nightmare, you must push back the limits, break the chains, squeeze every last fucking drop from it.

MARK: Do you have to curse so much?

STEVE: Fuck.

They run in silence.

MARK: (*Looking at his friend as if he doesn't recognise him.*) How did we ever get to know each other?

STEVE: Through a blowjob.

MARK: (*Confused.*) A blowjob?

STEVE: A blowjob from Francesca. We were at Alex's. Or Luke's. And you were going on about this party which you'd been at a few weeks before. I said I'd been there too. And I asked you if you remembered Francesca. Francesca? Course I remember Francesca, you said, didn't I snog her? Well, I said, didn't she give me a blowjob? What time did she give you a blowjob? you said. Round ten, I said. You went white: bitch, you said, I snogged her at ten-thirty –

STEVE laughs alone.

MARK: I don't remember that.

STEVE: That's typical. You never remember it when you steal my chick.

MARK: I stole Francesca from you?

STEVE: Francesca? Not Francesca. To hell with Francesca. Anna.

MARK: Anna. (*Bewildered.*) But... but that was ages back.

STEVE: Three years.

MARK: Whatever, three years. What difference does it make? You were the man. I even envied you. You could have had any girl you wanted.

STEVE: Not Anna.

MARK: But you said you didn't give a damn about her.

STEVE: Well, maybe I did.

STEVE runs on without speaking.

MARK: You saying you suffered in silence?

STEVE: Suffer*ed*?

MARK: You saying you still suffer? But we only lasted a few months.

STEVE: One year and two months.

MARK: Fuck, whatever. You never actually said anything.

STEVE: I don't like to be jealous. I didn't want to appear jealous.

MARK: So you'd rather poison three years of your life than appear to be jealous?

STEVE does not respond.

You prick.

Long silence.

You preferred to pretend you didn't care, rather than talk to me? You stupid, stupid prick.

STEVE: Yeah?

MARK: Yeah, you prick. Never thought you'd be one of those heads I'd want to run back in time to smash in.

STEVE: I should have smashed yours in.

MARK: We could fight about it now?

STEVE: What's the point. It's over.

MARK: (*Pause.*) I'm confused. I can't remember anything straight at the moment. Is that normal too, Steve?

STEVE: Forty-seven minutes; you've hyperoxygenated your brain, most likely.

MARK: What do you mean?

STEVE: Breathe slower and you'll feel better.

MARK: But it's not my breathing, it's my head. My head's so light. So light and clear. But clear like it's a wide open space. Desolate. And I feel like I'm not so much moving through it, but flying over it, just above the surface. Gliding –

STEVE: (*Preoccupied.*) What?

MARK: You were right, if you overcome your fear – I feel like I could go on forever. Why don't we pick up the pace?

STEVE: Our pace is fine.

MARK: I want to go faster.

STEVE: It's a mistake. You've got to know your limits.

MARK moves in front.

I'm serious. You'll push yourself too far. You could really fuck yourself up. You feel okay now, but it's just a passing moment. You'll hit the wall, Marko!

STEVE does his best to keep up with him.

You know I'm hurting and still you force the pace!

MARK does not relax his pace.

You going to help me out or not?

MARK does not respond.

First you have to be dragged along, then, when others need you –

STEVE loses ground. MARK does not bother to turn.

Have the Italian-Americans recognised me?

MARK does not respond.

What do they shout?

MARK: (*To himself.*) Go! Go! Go!

STEVE: Louder!

MARK: Go! Go! Go!

STEVE: Go! Go! Go! They encourage him, he grits his teeth. Raise the head. Calm the breathing. Look, he's recovering slightly. He digs in. He digs deep, he takes it like a man. He has the pride of a champion. Look, it's a miracle. He's back in the running.

STEVE recovers a little. But MARK remorselessly pulls away again.

Easy! Can't you see that I just can't do it?

MARK: How much has it taken for you to say that?

STEVE: I'll never help you out again. As soon as you feel better –

MARK: But I don't feel better. I'm cold. I'm cold, my legs are shaking.

STEVE: So why go faster?

MARK: All my life it's been the same.
    Others ran while I struggled to keep up
    the rear. I'd say to them: easy! Can't you
    see that I just can't do it? And they'd
    laugh at me. So I laughed at me too.
    That's me, a fucking joke. Once they
    locked me in the dressing room toilet for
    a joke; four fucking hours –

STEVE: What's that got to do with me?
    I never locked you in any toilet.

MARK: No, but you're always there pushing
    me, forcing the pace. And I'm always
    there, struggling to keep up the rear. Well,
    I don't want it anymore, you understand?

MARK speeds up.

STEVE: Look out, for Christ's sake, running
    like that's dangerous.

MARK: You say that because *you* are worried.

STEVE: I'm saying it because *you* could go
    off the road.

MARK: Another lecture.

STEVE: It's no joke. You're going too fast.

MARK speeds up once more.

Jesus, slow down.

MARK: I can't help it. My legs are going on their own.

STEVE: I can't keep up with you anymore.

MARK: I feel like the Greek guy.

STEVE: (*Desperately.*) The Greek guy was a stupid prick. When he arrived he couldn't even remember the message he had to bring.

MARK: I thought you said –

STEVE: What I said was just some stupid story.

Far away a car is heard to pass.

The moon has come closer, its light has become stronger. MARK is going very fast. STEVE progressively loses ground.

MARK: How long have we been running now?

STEVE: Fifty-nine minutes.

MARK: Including the break?

STEVE: Excluding.

MARK: Fifty-nine? It can't be. We haven't reached the level crossing.

STEVE: (*Sadly.*) You passed it.

MARK: I never saw it.

STEVE does not respond.

And you didn't say anything?

Silence.

MARK: We must turn back.

STEVE: You can't.

MARK: Why?

STEVE: You're going too fast.

MARK: (*Sniggering.*) Too fast! Me! (*Suddenly lost.*) But how come I'm so cold?

STEVE: You had the flu, remember.

MARK: Yeah... (*He is confused. Something puzzles him.*) And when we set off, why wasn't the car near us?

STEVE does not respond.

It must have been there. When we were doing our warm-up. But it wasn't. Why wasn't it there?

STEVE: You left it on the road.

MARK: Where?

STEVE: At the turn.

MARK: But I picked you up?

STEVE does not respond. He is exhausted and inconsolable.

And yet, I don't remember picking you up –

STEVE: One problem at a time, remember? Now's the time for running –

MARK: It's straight down the hill, and then, at the bottom, the turn. Fourth, down to third... I made it, Steve? I made the turn alright, Steve? Didn't I?

STEVE: Don't. There's no point, so don't.

MARK: Why?

STEVE: Because you're going like a dream. Don't think of anything else.

MARK: But I just thought of my mother. The way when I was little she'd raise the covers at the end of the bed and put my socks on my feet while I still pretended to sleep. Some days I'd be half-dressed before she'd lose all patience and shout at me. You know, it's suddenly struck me, I don't think she ever loved me.

STEVE: She loved you. Of course she loved you.

MARK: No, she didn't love what I really was. I was lazy, I always struggled to keep up the rear. She didn't love me. She loved you. Because we're brothers, aren't we Steve?

STEVE: We were, Marko. We were like brothers.

MARK: How come I'm thinking about my mother?

STEVE: Lengthen your stride. Open it up. Open it up – keep your breathing steady. You're doing an incredible time. You've never gone so fast. You're going to make it to New York. You're going to make it there tonight.

MARK speeds up even more. By now they have to shout to be heard by each other.

MARK: But, where are you?

STEVE: Here.

MARK: I can't see you anymore.

STEVE: There's a mist, don't you see?

MARK: But where are we? I don't recognise the landscape.

STEVE: Don't think about it. Run.

MARK: It's so cold.

STEVE: It's the frost.

MARK: What do you mean?

STEVE: The widespread frost.

MARK: Overtake me, please. I don't like being in front. I'm frightened.

STEVE: I can't. I've come this far, but now I've got to stop.

MARK: What? But you said you can't give up –

STEVE: You must go on alone. It's the way it is.

MARK: But the frost – I don't want to –

STEVE: I can't go with you any further.

MARK: Your spleen?

STEVE: My spleen's alright. I just can't come. Please understand.

They run in silence again for a bit.

MARK: Steve?

STEVE: Yes?

MARK: Were you with me in the car?

STEVE does not respond.

Tell me, Steve. I want to know.

STEVE: No, Marko, I wasn't. I stayed home to watch the match.

MARK: Oh Christ!

STEVE stops.

Why didn't you say before?

STEVE disappears into the dark. MARK runs on alone.

Do you forgive me, Steve? For Anna?
For being such a cunt sometimes?
For everything.

STEVE: (*From the dark.*) There's nothing to
forgive.

MARK: Look for the keys, give them to
my dad. They'll be in the wreckage –
they must be there somewhere.

MARK speeds up again, as if it was a sprint.

Steve? Stefano? What was the message I
had to bring?

The light disappears.

The End.

WWW.OBERONBOOKS.COM

Follow us on www.twitter.com/@oberonbooks
& www.facebook.com/OberonBooksLondon

Printed in the USA
CPSIA information can be obtained
at www.ICGtesting.com
LVHW021001171024
794056LV00004B/1281